Quick & Dirty
BOOKKEEPING

Complete a year's worth of

Accounting in a single afternoon

CRYSTAL WAMBEKE

ISBN-10: 0-692-92316-0
ISBN-13: 978-0-692-92316-0

Table of Contents

Chart of Accounts
Reports
Stop! Run Away

What You'll Need
Where You'll Find It
What You'll Do Next

Bank Loans (aka Liabilities)
Bank Interest
Transfers Between Accounts
Investments in the Business
Draws/Paychecks (aka Getting Paid)
Comingling of Business & Personal Funds
Refunds
Other Revenue
Other Expenses
Employees vs. Contractors

Keep Growing
Know Your Numbers
Think, "Money's Sexy!"
Avoid Tax Time Panic

DEDICATION

This book is dedicated to my husband Michael. Thanks for being tirelessly supportive, for making me laugh, for always applauding my nerdy tendencies and for believing I can move the Earth. (You make me believe it, too.) I love you like crazy. It's also dedicated to a long list of people (see "Acknowledgements"). Among them is our dog, Jack — the world's coziest foot warmer. And to you, the weekend warrior who's bound and determined to get your bookkeeping done. *It's time we rock those financials!*

PREFACE

Do you constantly struggle with your bookkeeping?

Business owners and bookkeepers alike often tell me that they spend so much time trying to figure out their books that they don't seem to have time to do anything else. Either that or they struggle to the point where they end up putting off "for tomorrow" what can—literally—be done in an afternoon. Yep, you heard me right: a single afternoon.

It's not uncommon for business owners to push against the current, when it comes to getting or keeping their books in order. They get so frustrated by the sheer volume of receipts and bank statements they've accumulated that they simply give up. Yet, giving up doesn't come naturally to entrepreneurs. It's understandably frustrating for them (and for you, I'm guessing) to leave that stone unturned.

As a Certified Bookkeeper, I see it all too often.

They get so busy running and building their businesses that they decide to tackle their bookkeeping tasks at a later date. Maybe tomorrow. Or the next day. Or the week after that. When they finally do come back around to it months later, they still haven't gained any clarity. This makes things even more stressful, jumpstarting the cycle of procrastination all over again.

Business owners of all types and in all industries believe they should update their books on a regular basis. Yet, they routinely ignore them until they're presented with an IRS deadline. Sound familiar? If this describes you, stop a minute and breathe a sigh of relief: You're not alone! Waiting until the last minute to get your paperwork in order is a common problem among business owners and individuals.

Like clockwork, April 15th comes around each year. In the interim, we get so busy running our businesses and homes that we fail to pay attention to our finances until we're left without any other choice. With 70 percent of all businesses in America run as sole proprietorships, LLCs or partnerships, I'm here to tell you that your accounting needs probably aren't as complicated as you think they are.

This book proves it. You don't need a fancy degree and you don't have to hire an expensive accounting firm to get your bookkeeping done on a regular basis. In fact, by making time to regularly update your books, you can save yourself a lot of time, money and worry. Sure, a fancy degree and an expensive accounting firm are ideal, if you run a complex business with lots of unique financial concerns.

If that were the case, I seriously doubt you'd be reading this.

What you'll learn on the following pages is informed by my own experience as an Accountant, Certified Bookkeeper and small business owner who's worked with small to mid-sized businesses since 2007. I'll take you from the Bookkeeping Abyss to Accounting Land and back again, sharing simple tips which will make keeping your financials in order a way of life you can wrap your head around — and begin using now.

It's nice to have you along for the ride. Let's get started!

INTRODUCTION

This book assumes that you use an electronic accounting system of some kind. That may take the form of software you bought (or plan to buy) at an office supply or big box store, a cloud-based accounting program or a basic Excel spreadsheet. It also assumes that, to at least some extent, you've already researched and begun implementing an accounting system that helps you keep track of your finances.

If not, Chapter 3 outlines a few different types of accounting programs which are available to you. It also offers basic guidelines for deciding which ones may best suit your wants and needs. If you hadn't yet considered setting up a computer-based accounting system, I suggest that you rethink the idea of sticking with pen and paper—i.e., a ledger, in which you record and then tally money in/out.

If you choose to keep paper records, much of this book won't pertain to you. More importantly, you'll miss out on critical opportunities to ensure that your financial data and bookkeeping system are: efficient, accurate and capable of being sorted for analysis at the press of a button or two. That alone is great reason to invest in even the most rudimentary accounting software program.

Since technology changes and improves incredibly quickly, I won't spend much time explaining how to use any specific platform. I also resist promoting one over the others. They all have their strengths and only you can determine which makes the most sense. A quick internet search will lead you to a dozen or more articles on how each platform is set up, how they function and how to arrive at the best possible fit.

Instead, I'll use this book to provide you with expert bookkeeping tips and leave the tasks of dishing out technical advice to someone who's better qualified. (You'll thank me later!) Together, we'll focus on things like how to do your bookkeeping. Especially if you'd rather be doing a million other things. You'll come to find that, unlike technology, the fundamental rules of accounting don't change much.

That, in itself, takes a big weight off of your shoulders. Let's celebrate with a sigh of relief: *Ahhh!*

I want you to walk away with a cursory understanding of those rules. I want you to know that you can work your way out of the Bookkeeping Abyss, using any bookkeeping tool your heart desires. I want you to be able to easily find your way through Accounting Land. Will there be a learning curve? Sure, particularly when it comes to mastering electronic tools, programs and platforms you're unfamiliar with.

As you'll see — in Chapters 4, 5 and elsewhere — there are also accounting methods, transaction types and other complications to deal with. Yet? I have confidence in you and, ahem, in my own ability to make things easy on you. Unlike an accounting textbook, this book is specifically designed to provide basic instruction that'll help you conquer months' worth of bookkeeping in a single afternoon. It's that simple.

I also know how helpful it is to have access to templates and sample information, so I've made an entire portal on my website where you can download a bunch of great information. Head over to www.crystalwambeke.com and check it out.

This book won't change who you are or inspire you to love bookkeeping. But, hey, if it does? I want to know about it. What it will do is get you out of a jam. If a particular passage seems irrelevant or too advanced, skip over it. If others seem so obvious you wonder why I'm wasting time on them, feel free to once again skip ahead. What I try to do, throughout, is get to the point so you can get on with your day.

If you need to get your books done ASAP and want step-by-step instructions, here they are.

Crystal Wambeke
Owner of Crystal Wambeke, LLC
Accountant & Certified Bookkeeper

P.S. – I'd love to know how this book has helped you! Email me via Crystal@CrystalWambeke.com.

CHAPTER 1. WHY ME?

I didn't always want to be an Accountant.

In fact, working as an Accountant or anything even remotely related to it was the furthest thing from my mind. Shoot, I nearly failed H.S. Accounting. (Thanks to a sympathetic teacher, I passed that course.) Then it was off to college. Did I graduate? Sure, though not with an Accounting degree. When unexpectedly asked if I'd like to take a job as an Accounting Assistant, I thought, "What's the worst that can happen?"

Short on accounting knowledge but rich in imagination, it took just a quick second to envision the worst-case scenario: I'd wind up ruining everything! I'd surely put minus signs where they didn't belong, forget to add important numbers together and single-handedly bankrupt an entire government institution. Yes, I was certain that the U.S. President would then be compelled to call me and tell me that I was the worst thing to ever happen to our country, promising that I'd never land another job. *Ever!*

"What's the worst that can happen?"

Well, the worst never did happen. Instead, I learned that I was actually pretty good at this accounting stuff. I was debiting all the right things, creating spreadsheets that added up the way they were designed to and using related jargon like a seasoned professional might. It was great! (I was even promoted pretty quickly.) Yet, I soon realized I had too much time on my hands and an overabundance of ambition. That's when I began searching for a part-time job that would occupy my weekends.

My boss had given me a lead on a company that was looking for a P/T Bookkeeper, so landing that gig was easy—plus I loved it. That led to a string of temporary, or otherwise part-time, bookkeeping positions. While it happened slowly, I was becoming an entrepreneur. Soon enough, it was "Ta-da!" My business was born and I found myself on a mission to help other small businesses meet their bookkeeping needs. If I'm being totally honest with you, I have to say that I knew I'd be a great asset to them.

On top of being good at bookkeeping for a variety of business types, I had a unique perspective and understood what it was like to not know much about bookkeeping in the first place. I'd begun my own career knowing pretty much nothing about bookkeeping and accounting. If I could learn to understand and master them, I knew I could help other people do the same. So, I set out to do just that with a Vision Statement that read: *I help business owners become rock stars at doing their own books.*

The thought of being my own boss was also extremely appealing.

Despite having a clear goal in mind, I still had a few things to learn. I decided to return to college and was accepting into a Master of Professional Accountancy (or M.P.Acy.) program. At the same time, I began pursuing and earned a Certified Bookkeeper designation from the American Institute of Professional Bookkeepers. I did that to prove to myself that I was truly ready for "the big time," having known that the testing process was pretty rigorous. All that was left to do was officially open for business.

Non-traditional as that pathway was, it's how I came to run my own bookkeeping agency. The services I offer include, but often go beyond: bookkeeping for small businesses, training business owners in basic accounting and bookkeeping principles, training those business owners' in-house bookkeeping teams in the finer points of accounting and bookkeeping, leading small group or community-based seminars and workshops which help regular folks understand the ins-and-outs of bookkeeping, etc.

While most of the business owners I meet have a basic understanding of how their own books work, few are experienced in doing any bookkeeping. They're also slightly, if not highly, uncomfortable with the idea of tackling their books themselves. They realize they're not specialists and know that businesses like mine exist solely for the purpose of providing them with bookkeeping services. What's more, most businesses offer a product or service that has nothing to do with accounting. Not directly, anyway.

Bookkeeping tasks represent a tiny fraction of what it is those companies and their owners are already worried about. There are marketing plans to put in place. There are new government regulations to come into compliance with. There are products and services to manufacture, bundle together and sell. Doing the books routinely becomes one more thing they're responsible for — and it's one thing they pretty much all wind up putting off for far too long. The reason for that? A lack of knowledge.

Most people simply don't know where to begin. It's not enough to worry that you'll miss something or do something wrong. On top of it all, they worry that one wrong move could end up inadvertently sinking their entire companies. This level of apprehension is normal and practically a rite of passage for business owners who didn't major in accounting. Still, I promise you, this book is a great first step toward making sure your worst fears don't materialize.

As it turns out, I happen to know what I'm talking about.

In the course of running my own company, I've found that I am extremely talented in the art of fixing other people's messy bookkeeping mistakes. It's also why I see a need for a book like this. Time and time again I receive phone calls from people who say, "Help! I didn't do my books at all last year and I need to get my stuff to the CPA who does my taxes." Without exception, they're all in a panic — stressed over where to start and confused about what it is their CPA needs from them.

I enjoy helping people out of these situations and I love my job. Sometimes, though, business owners like you just want to know how to do their books themselves. And quickly! What they don't know is how and where to start the process. None of them can seem to find a book or a video on the topic that isn't confusing, cumbersome or expensive. Since "easy, fast and affordable" is largely a unicorn request (especially come crunch time), they end up hiring me or someone like me to do the work for them.

Depending on how much lead time they provide, how disorganized their existing recordkeeping method is and how long it will take me to get everything shipshape, providing them with help can quickly teeter over into "complex, slow-moving and expensive" territory. In reality? I trust they could do their books themselves, if they were given appropriate instruction, sound advice and basic guidance. Heck, I'm confident I can teach you to master your own books and have written this title with you in mind.

In *Quick & Dirty Bookkeeping*, I'll guide you through a set of accounting basics every small business owner should know about. I'll help you catch up on last year's books in the course of an afternoon. I'll even introduce you to accounting platforms which can make life easier going forward. In the process, I'll clear away confusion over the bookkeeping concerns which commonly plague small business owners. Some of it is advanced stuff you'd normally need a CPA's help with, but I may as well spill the beans here.

I'll help you catch up on last year's books in the course of an afternoon.

What do you need? An accounting system, an afternoon free, an open mind—and perhaps some coffee!

CHAPTER 2.
HELP! WHAT ARE THESE NUMBERS?
(And Why Are They Called the Books? Seriously, Why?)

I can see you scratching your head. Well, OK, I can't actually see you from where I'm sitting. Still, I can imagine it and I don't blame you. What are all those numbers you see staring back at you from within that glowing, white, electronic spreadsheet? How are you supposed to use them? And don't you need formal training to do your bookkeeping? Heck, why's it called doing "the books," anyway? Seriously ... why?

Let's start at the beginning, so you'll understand what we're doing here. Bookkeeping got its name a long time ago—when business accounts were reconciled in large, leather-bound ledger books. Back then computers didn't exist and everything was done by hand. Their pages sported lines and columns and rows. They looked like pages in a checkbook register or spreadsheet but on a much larger scale.

Notebook-sized versions of these ledgers can still be found in office supply stores.

Lots of people still use them, in cases where whole accounting systems aren't necessary. A seamstress who picks up odd jobs might use one to keep track of the mad money she earns. An amateur woodworker who builds custom bookends in his home-based workshop may keep one around for tracking expenses and money earned. The term "the books" derives from the act of tracking finances in ledgers.

A few other variants, which are used interchangeably in everyday language, include:

- The Numbers
- The Financials
- Financial Data
- Keeping the Books
- Number Crunching

One term we'll use extensively here is "the numbers." This information is found in your bookkeeping records and is usually arrived at by running one of those weird reports your electronic accounting system is able to produce with the click of a button. Being able to run one of these fancy reports has the power to make you feel as if you've just pulled a rabbit out of a magic hat. That is, once you get the hang of it!

S.O.S. Received

When I speak with someone who's new to accounting, their first words are often, "Help me!" They are lost and they think of accounting as a super complicated process. What they're lacking is perspective and clarity. Yes, their books are usually a mess. However, they too often chalk that up to their prior, failed attempts at bookkeeping solo. Here's a typical plea:

> "I know this stuff is important. I just don't know why. I tried to do my books, made a mess and can't seem to get it right. I have bags full of receipts and bank statements and overdue customer invoices. What am I supposed to do with all of this stuff? Trying to make sense of these spreadsheets is like trying to read Mandarin. And, I mean, I barely made it through H.S. Spanish. Please, I beg you. Help me!" — Actual Client *
>
> (* = *Not his real name, as I sought to spare him further embarrassment.*)

See? You're not alone! Maybe it feels as if you're in this man's shoes. I know I've been there. So have lots of other people. Right now, all you know for sure is that "accounting" is a scary word, there are a lot of numbers involved and none of the lingo makes sense. (Not yet, anyway.) You could even be feeling a bit frustrated or overwhelmed, if you've already suffered a few false starts. That's a natural reaction.

I'd feel the same way, if you suddenly threw open the shutters on your own business and asked me if I wanna have a go at it. Like anything, though, accounting is a *learned* skill — like computer programming, car repair or landscaping. I know how to surf the web. I can fill my own gas tank. And I certainly admire plants! Does that mean I can build websites, replace head gaskets and grow tomatoes? Uh, no.

With the exception of maybe the tomatoes, none of those tasks comes naturally to me.

I'd need to learn a few basics before I'd feel comfortable tackling them and doing any one of them would take more effort than bookkeeping currently requires of me. Conversely, you may be a whiz at coding, engine repair or gardening. In any case, this book won't turn you into a bookkeeper. (Poof!) What it will do is teach you how to keep basic books. For most folks? That's more than enough!

Why Should I Care?

QUESTION: What do these (10) things have in common?

- Taking a salary
- Paying your bills
- Hiring employees
- Applying for a loan
- Growing your business
- Opening another location
- Renegotiating with suppliers
- Managing overhead expenses
- Filing annual or quarterly taxes
- Maintaining adequate inventory

ANSWER: Your books. You guessed it, didn't you? (I knew you'd catch on quickly!)

Have you ever watched that TV show? The one where people pitch their ideas to investors who battle it out to decide who'll give them HUGE sums of money and 1-on-1 mentoring which then helps them develop and grow their businesses? Or the other one — where the expert consultant shows up, shakes things to their core and makes businesses profitable again? If so, you know where this is headed.

After getting a sense for what the organization does and who runs it, the first thing those experts ask for is the company's numbers. Those investors and advisors know that the only way to assess whether or not a business has the potential to be successful is by reviewing its financials. You're clearly savvy to the power of financial data. After all, you're here learning to crunch your own numbers. "Bravo," I say!

Is This Gonna Hurt?

If you expect to effectively carry out even one of the ten functions listed above, your books need to be up-to-date. If you have your sights set on doing any of the myriad other things entrepreneurs and small business owners find exciting, your numbers must add up. If you make it onto one of those TV shows (stranger things have happened), you'd better hope your books are in order.

What's more, keeping your books in order needn't be a pain in the—oh, don't make me say it!

More importantly, if done right, doing your bookkeeping can be downright rewarding. Don't believe me? Here are five great ways you can use your updated numbers to make your business even more profitable. If they don't motivate you to at least fall "in like" with your financials, I don't know what will.

(5) Great Uses for Up-to-Date Numbers

- **Identify trends.** – Celebrate upswings and work to reverse lulls.
- **Monitor sales goals.** – Use these details to adjust your sales strategy.
- **Prevent overspending.** – Keep the impulse to spend in check with real data.

- **Track department budgets.** – Look back, identifying who needs what and when.
- **Make adjustments accordingly.** – If all goes well, give yourself (and others) a raise.

No wonder millionaire entrepreneurs and successful CEOs know their numbers. Soon? You will, too!

That said, not everyone's motivated by money. I get that. In fact, I often hear something along these lines: "I have enough money in the bank to pay my bills each month and to buy more inventory. So, why should I bother with bookkeeping? I mean, what's the point? I feel as if I'm already successful enough and I'm actually glad I don't have to spend a good chunk of my time worrying about every financial detail."

Believe it or not, this is a fairly common mindset. Although the thought behind it is incomplete, it is not completely wrong. If you have enough money in the bank to make payroll, order inventory and pay your utility bills? Well, that's great! You're on your way to success. However, having money in the bank does not mean your business is profitable. And this is the point at which many people trip themselves up.

Yes, profit is loosely defined as an excess of revenue over expenses. Plainly speaking it means that you earned more than you spent in a given period of time. Before you think, "Duh, Crystal! That's why I have money in the bank. My business is profitable. I already told you that!" let me clarify. Bookkeeping *verifies* those numbers, ensuring that no bit of critical data has been overlooked.

The only way to verify a profit is through careful tracking of your actual Expenses and Income.

One Last Detail

Let's cover one last detail before we move forward.

Are you using the Cash or Accrual method? When filing income tax forms, you're often asked the very same question. I've written this book with the assumption that you, like the majority of my business clients, use a cash-based accounting method. That's because my primary goal is to help you spend less time doing your books and not more. In that regard, cash is king.

Accrual-based accounting systems can be used with the principles I present here. However, there are details of that method which are too intricate to cover in this book. To illustrate their differences, I'll guide you through a simple revenue-and-expense situation. If you need help making a decision between the two or simply want to know more, shoot me an email.

The Situation: Cash vs. Accrual Accounting

On January 1, you Special Order an item for one of your customers. They need it quickly, so you request Express shipment from the manufacturer. On January 2, you receive it. Enclosed is an invoice dated January 1 but marked NET90. You have 90 days from January 1 to pay the manufacturer. Later that day, your customer picks up the item. You hand them an invoice marked NET60. They have 60 days from January 2 to pay you. As it turns out, they pay you in February and you pay your vendor in April.

The Outcome: A Quick & Dirty Comparison

The way you'll account for related expenses and revenue, as outlined in the following scenarios — one representing the Cash method and one representing the Accrual method — differs. This explanation of outcomes is designed to give you a basic primer in the fundamentals of each method.

Cash method

In February, your customer paid you for an item they received in January. The revenue generated by that sale will, therefore, be recognized in your numbers for February. If you charged them $100, that $100 will be counted as "Business Revenue" earned in February.

Since you waited until April to pay the manufacturer for the item, your cost to purchase it will appear in your books as an April expense, coinciding with the date you paid for it. Under the Cash method, you'll account for expenses or revenue-generating transactions as they come to pass.

This method is easily understood and applied, which is why small businesses often use it.

Accrual method

This method is more complex, so bear with me. Accrual accounting methods operate on a sort of timeline which requires that transactions are recorded upfront, in sync with the original time of sale. In "The Situation" outlined above, your bookkeeping records for January—versus February and April, as with the Cash method—are where entries for the transactions above would appear.

The first would show up as an expense incurred on January 1 and the second as revenue generated on January 2. That's true despite the NET90 and NET60 terms associated with them. Until money is exchanged, those transactions will continue to show up as due on your books.

The revenue generator will appear as an "Accounts Receivable" item (what's owed to you) until February. The initial expense will appear as an "Accounts Payable" item (what you owe others) until April. With Accrual, a sale was made and an expense is owed.

You're now tracking both items: One for receipt and one for payment.

Cash vs. Accrual

- Cash – Transactions are recorded on the date money changes hands.
- Accrual – Transactions are recorded upon origination and are tracked as either "Accounts Receivable" or "Accounts Payable" items until their status is resolved.

As if all of that weren't confusing enough, some businesses use a Modified Cash system. This allows them to use a cash-basis accounting method but still keep track of Accounts Receivable, which does help generate more accurate reports.

Are you ready to start hittin' the books? Me, too! Let's move on to the topic of software.

CHAPTER 3.
DECISIONS, DECISIONS

When it comes to electronic bookkeeping, there are many options. We'll discuss a few here.

At the beginning of this book, I promised to introduce you to a few accounting platforms which might make life easier; specifically, the part of your life that's spent avoiding tasks like bookkeeping. I also pointed out that this book assumes that you use some electronic method for tracking your numbers. That's either a cloud-based or desktop software program you use to record and store your financial data.

Old school ledger books will not suffice for use with this book. So, it's time you decide between:

- Desktop Accounting Software
- Cloud-Based Programs
- Excel Spreadsheets
- -&- Outsourcing

Methods for helping you keep your books up-to-date are as diverse as the various industries they're designed to serve. Keep reading to arrive at the best decision for your individual situation.

Desktop Accounting Software

If you and perhaps one or two other people in your office are the only ones who need access to your books, desktop accounting software is a great option. Once downloaded it will prompt you to answer questions about your business, further customizing your initial set up. This is a good choice for companies which have one central location and don't require access to accounting files outside of business hours.

Pros:

- Initial software package is a one-time purchase
- Usually accommodate various levels of accounting
- Contractor, wholesaler and supplier platforms available
- Easily backed up on a local computer or external hard drive

Cons:

- Upfront investment may be expensive
- Program updates often have a fee attached
- With files saved locally, there's no remote access
- Sometimes too robust or complex for basic business use

At the time of this printing, the primary industry standards are:

- QuickBooks
- Quicken
- Sage

QuickBooks

QuickBooks (desktop version) is a widely used platform with advanced accounting capabilities. Offered by Intuit, it is geared toward businesses which might benefit from accounting systems with broad functionality and semi-intuitive menus. While the reporting feature—or, the aspect of the accounting software system which lets you sort data and generate reports—is expansive, it is also relatively easy to use.

Quicken

Quicken is a basic, DIY platform tailored around the light business and personal user. This is a great beginner's tool, as this software program is designed specifically for those who aren't power users. Though it's also currently offered by Intuit, there is little overlap between Quicken and QuickBooks, so don't confuse the two. The reporting section is basic and user-friendly.

Sage

Sage may be best suited to businesses which require accounting software systems with advanced reporting features and a great ability to capture details. It is robust and has high reporting functionality. It's not, therefore, an advisable choice for the novice bookkeeper. That said, what it lacks in ease-of-use it makes up for with extended capabilities.

Cloud-Based Programs

Cloud-based accounting programs aren't saved to your local computer. Rather, files are saved to a cloud network and the programs themselves are accessed online. This is a great option for anyone who needs to access their bookkeeping files from virtually anywhere. It's also ideal if you need to share access or records with multiple users. If you employ a virtual accountant in a different time zone or have a business partner in another state, this may be your best option. There are usually companion mobile apps, as well.

Pros:

- Off-site storage and file keeping
- 24/7 remote and multi-user access

- Mobile app and automatic update features
- Usually less complex than desktop software

Cons:

- Lack of ownership over product
- Recurring, monthly fees to subscribe
- Cloud-based-only storage of data
- Less robust or complex (i.e., fewer accounting functions)

At the time of this printing, the primary industry standards are:

- QuickBooks
- Wave
- Xero

QuickBooks

QuickBooks Online is a cloud-based equivalent to the desktop version. It trades some functionality for convenience but generally ranks high as an industry standard. If you know your way around the desktop version's menus, adopting this cloud-based solution will be easy for you. It is relatively easy-to-use, straightforward and has an appealing design. While this version may be light on inventory management capabilities (for those who need them), it does offer a good range of reporting functionalities.

Wave

The Wave platform (as of this printing, available at no charge) may be best suited to small businesses that are just starting out or have light-duty accounting needs. Its functionality is relatively basic, though it can be used to run a standard selection of reports. What sets this option apart is its inclusion of a Personal Finance portal, through which individual income and expenses can also be tracked.

Xero

Though it functions similarly to Wave, Xero is more advanced. I happen to know various folks who prefer Xero over any other accounting platform. That's not because it's ultrachic or even expensive. Those who do so prefer it because its menus operate nearly opposite other popular options. (In some circles, it's regarded as the "Anti-QuickBooks.") While it delivers fewer reporting options and its menus aren't terribly intuitive, it gets the job done. So, in the realm of cloud-based accounting software, it's definitely worth considering.

Excel Spreadsheets

A simple Microsoft Excel spreadsheet can sometimes be the perfect solution for tracking expenses, revenues, etc. It's a practical choice for anyone who doesn't need a lot of fancy features, such as a small business owner who conducts a minimal number of monthly transactions and doesn't require full-blown accounting software. Related spreadsheet data can be sorted and compiled into a range of basic reports.

Pros:

- Spreadsheets are relatively easy-to-use
- Low cost, as it's often pre-loaded on some devices
- Optional cloud-based storage offers 24/7 remote access

Cons:

- Spreadsheets must be set up from scratch
- Not robust enough to handle complex accounting
- Financial reports have to be configured and run manually

Outsourcing

WARNING! Never shirk your responsibility, as a business owner, and always pay attention.

I never know how to react when business owners tell me things like: "I have a person who comes in three days a week to help me. They take out the trash, pay the bills, design marketing flyers and answer the phones. Sometimes they even bring me cookies! I'll just have *them* do my books. That way I'll never have to learn to do it myself. Mwah-ha-ha-ha-ha!" Uh, sure. That could work out well. (Or not.)

I'm a firm believer in outsourcing tasks you aren't suited to tackle yourself, which is a common practice. Heck, my business is built on the notion of outsourced bookkeeping. Not only am I a person who does work for others. I also like to outsource work of my own that's better done by someone else. I outsource my car maintenance and dental care as I am — without a doubt — unqualified to do either.

Outsourcing tasks you don't want to tackle yourself is common practice

Still, while I don't flush transmissions for a living, I know how the task is completed.

Similarly, I may not take a drill to my back molar but I know what method my dentist will use to address that problem. I get involved because I care about my car. And my teeth! They're mine and I want to know what's happening to them. It's also my money I'm spending on maintenance or upkeep. So, I want to be sure I'm getting my money's worth and am only authorizing those things which are in my best interest.

Being informed allows me to ask better questions, advocate from a position of control over my things and prevent breakdowns in communication, car parts or cavities. Being informed also acts as a barrier to being taken advantage of. If I weren't prone to paying attention, I might be taken to the cleaners by someone who offers to overhaul my engine for $10,000 when all I need is a refill on windshield wiper fluid.

Do you see what I'm getting at? Ultimately, I'm responsible for my own car, teeth and financials.

Likewise, you should always be mindful of your financial situation. You can do that, when outsourcing, by sitting down with your bookkeeper or accountant on a regular basis. This helps you ensure that any professional you hire to maintain your financials is acting responsibly and has a firm grasp of what your business goals are. It also helps you stay abreast of potential issues and take timely, corrective action.

Your business and its financial health are ultimately your responsibility. No one else's. Ignoring your finances is like ignoring the ticking of an engine. It'll come back to bite you in the long run. If you don't want to do your bookkeeping yourself, outsource it. But do take time to learn a few bookkeeping basics.

Reading this book is a great first step. Engaging in "Responsible Outsourcing" is another.

(5) Tips for Responsible Outsourcing

- Do your fair share of the workload.
- Keep up-to-date invoices, receipts, etc.
- Develop a logical, organized filing system.
- Know what you owe and what's owed to you.
- Schedule quarterly meetings with your bookkeeper.

Once your financials are in order, you may just decide to maintain your books in-house.

You're always welcome to choose that option. The benefits of doing your own books include an ability to get updates in real time. You can also spot trends or potential problem areas of critical importance; ones which may not wave around like a red flag to someone outside of your industry who was simply hired to crunch numbers. If your situation is complicated, expert bookkeeping or accounting help makes sense.

Referral Sources May Include:

- CPA or peer recommendations
- Freelance exchanges (i.e., Upwork, oDesk)
- Industry websites (i.e., AIPB.org, NACPB.org, AAAHQ.org)

- Good old search engines (i.e., Google, Yelp, Merchant Circle)

One final word on outsourcing. To maintain good dental health I must brush, floss and avoid opening soda cans with my teeth. If I neglect to do the first two and opt instead to routinely do the third, I just may end up living with a cavity. Or worse, as in a mouthful of broken teeth. You've got your own responsibilities to tend to. A full set of choppers or something close to it. A car, perhaps. Maybe a family and a dog. Do what you can to maintain them.

Hire help, as needed, but know that the buck stops with you. Literally!

CHAPTER 4.
ACCOUNTING BASICS
(Or, Simply, How Bookkeeping Works)

If you want to know the basic principles behind bookkeeping, read on!

This chapter takes you on a trip through the fundamentals of basic accounting so that you can fully understand how bookkeeping works. As a side effect, you'll also learn how keeping things in order can benefit you. If you don't have the time to learn this right now or already have a general understanding of these concepts, feel free to jump to Chapter 6. (That's where the really good stuff begins!)

Adventures in Accounting Land

Whether we're talking about your financials or how to give a facial, I'm a firm believer in understanding the big picture before drilling down into the details. By teaching you the basic functions of bookkeeping and rules of accounting, I plan to make you more comfortable with the idea of doing your books yourself.

Once you understand how they function, you'll be able to apply those rules using any accounting system you like. You'll also be able to use the fancy jargon outlined below to wow potential investors.

Our first stop is a place I like to call Accounting Land.

It's like a theme park—minus the exciting rides, larger-than-life characters, overpriced food and oversized drinks. Hmmm, I guess it's not so much like a theme park after all. Anyway, Accounting Land is great! It's where people communicate in numbers, describe things using acronyms (or other snazzy abbreviations) and use strange words which seem to have sprung from a made-up language. You'll hear "transaction," "expenditure" and "depreciation" regularly.

A calculator is mandatory. A dry sense of humor? Optional.

While this may all seem a bit weird now, once you get the hang of the park rules it'll seem pretty darned fun. (You'll have to trust me on this one.) We'll begin by reviewing some basic terminology, which will make navigating your way through Accounting Land a breeze. After all, I can't be your tour guide forever. Though, come to think of it, you can always email me if you get lost. Think you can handle this? I know you can. Strap yourself in, 'cause here we go!

Words Worth Knowing

No one makes it through Accounting Land without learning a few choice words. Words you can throw around at cocktail parties, bar mitzvahs and bridal showers. After all, who's gonna stop you? Acquiring a taste for this kind of terminology isn't as tricky as you might expect. In fact, it's a rite of passage—like flailing your arms in the air while riding a massive roller coaster at your favorite amusement park.

OK, enough with the hard sell. Let's start expanding your vocabulary!

Transaction

> In Accounting Land, the word "transaction" is used to describe the act of buying or selling goods or services. Every time money comes in or goes out, a transaction has taken place. Let's say you lay down money for a lemonade delivered in a souvenir cup. You've just completed a transaction! Let's say you then return it, citing a broken straw. That's *another* transaction. Along those same lines, each entry on your bank statement represents a transaction (i.e., debit, credit, interest earned). You'll need to remember this word later, so get comfortable with it.

Revenue

Revenue is money earned. (Yes, it's that simple!)

Expenditure

An expenditure is money spent.

Financial Records

This is the point where we begin to pull everything together. In Accounting Land, every single revenue and expense transaction must be tracked. (← See what I did there? Now you're thinking like an accountant.) "But, Crystal," you say, "what does tracking mean?" Tracking is the organization of your incoming and outgoing money, using a method that allows you to then review it. However, to review that data it must appear together in one place. Soon I'll teach you to gather it up in one place and organize it. For now just know that "Financial Records" are formal documents which are used to outline those collective business transactions.

Accounting Database

In Accounting Land, we keep all financial records in either a spreadsheet, an electronic software system or on paper. This is what's called your "Accounting Database" or "Accounting Information System." As was noted earlier, you'll need to set up on electronic accounting system of some sort before you can take any of the major steps outlined in this book. See Chapter 3 for help selecting the best method (i.e., Excel, Quicken, Xero), according to your individual needs.

These are the primary terms you need to know upfront. You'll learn others, as we move through the bookkeeping process. Next, we'll take a look at how accounting rules function. Believe it or not, doing that speeds up the process of getting a handle on your accounting software, database or information system.

Buckets o' Money

Once the revenue and expenditure transactions you want to track are safely tucked away in your electronic accounting database, you need to organize them. In its simplest form, that requires sorting and then lumping like transactions into different, virtual buckets o' money. This is done so that reports can be run. Those reports then give us a big-picture view of the overall health of our businesses. I don't know about you, but I like to think of this organization stuff in terms of a game.

Let's Play the Bucket Game!

If you were born before 1985, you might remember a TV show that was hosted by a clown.

On it, kids were able to play games and have fun. One of those games was the Bucket Game. To win, contestants had to successfully throw ping pong balls into a bucket. That's how I want you to think about organizing your transactions. The next time you spend money on your business, pick the bucket that best describes the transaction type and throw that information inside it.

It makes sense to lump all business vehicle expense transactions into an "Auto Expenses" bucket. Oil changes. Tune ups. Tire rotations. Engine overhauls. Let's hope it doesn't come to that last one. But, if it does, at least your accounting database will be equipped to handle it. Every related expense transaction would be captured in the same, convenient location. Likewise, it makes sense to gather all of your sales and revenue data (that is, your earnings) into a "Sales Income" bucket. See how this works?

Organizing transactions of a similar nature into well-labeled buckets is the grown-up equivalent of the Bucket Game. The payoff is well worth the price of admission to Accounting Land. After this process is complete, you can direct your software to run a report that tells you exactly how much money you have earned or spent during a given time frame. The resulting numbers will be broken down neatly and summarized by transaction type—or bucket.

In real life, those buckets are called "Accounts." Accounts provide structure and organization. They function as the heart of your books, really. They're essential to the tasks of retrieving and then gleaning understandable information from your books. They also make it possible to keep your financials in order and to make sense of large quantities of numeric data with relative ease.

Of course, you have a role to play in all of this. That's what we'll dive into next!

(5) Primary Account Types

Knowing that accounts are categories you sort transactions into isn't enough. Accounting rules dictate that, in the course of keeping your books, five primary account types must always be accounted for: *Assets, Expenses, Liabilities, Revenue* and *Equity*.

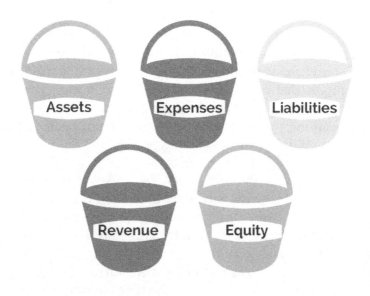

We'll review each one below. While your company will certainly require more than five measly buckets to divvy its transactions into, no matter how many you add each bucket will fall within one of those five categories or account types. In other words, they'll serve as sub-accounts to those main accounts.

Assets

I'm sure you've heard this word thrown around in daily life. If you've ever applied for a loan, you were probably asked if you possessed "assets" which could be put up for collateral against the value of the proposed loan. Assets, it turns out, are things you own. That applies in business, too, which is why businesses strive to have lots and lots of assets. Typical business assets include:

- Cash and Investments
- Equipment or Product Inventory
- Checking and Savings Account Balances
- Accounts Receivable (aka money customers owe you)
- Fixed Assets (i.e., furniture, computers, buildings, land)

Expenses

Expenses are things you spend money on. It's that straight-forward. Examples include:

- Utilities
- Other Bills

- Payroll Expenses
- Inventory Purchases
- Day-to-Day Operating Costs

Liabilities

I bet you've heard this term thrown around, as well. Liabilities are debts you owe. When you take a loan or a line of credit, the money due becomes a liability to you. Adding debts to your financials allows you—and your investors—to quickly track them, getting an at-a-glance look at what your business is liable for and is required to repay.

- Taxes Due
- Bank Loans
- Credit Card Debt
- Inventory Lines of Credit
- Accounts Payable (i.e., money you owe vendors)

Revenue

Mentioned earlier, revenue is money earned. "Money earned in the normal course of business," mind you, is just fancy accountant speak for money earned while doing what it is your business is intended to do. If you're a hair stylist, that means styling hair. If you're a builder, it means building. Here are a few other common sources of business revenue:

- Service Fees
- Consulting Fees
- Merchandise Sales
- Broker Fees Earned
- Referral Commissions

I want to stress that revenue DOES NOT include bank-issued interest or any of the following. These types of deposits are *unusual* and *rarely occur*. They are typically classified as liabilities or fall under a separate account type labeled "Other Revenue," showing up in your financial reports as money received but NOT from doing normal business:

- Insurance Payouts
- Money Found on the Street
- Bank or Credit Line Advances
- Crowdsourcing Campaign Funds
- Money Gained in a Lawsuit Settlement

If your life is impacted by one of these situations, you'll probably want to get some expert help. Anyone who reads your reports will need to know to distinguish between money your business earned from its customers and money your business took in from sources like these. There really is a HUGE difference. If you're curious to know more about these and other "Complications," you can always flip to Chapter 7.

Equity

Equity is funding contributed by shareholders. "Retained earnings" also falls within this category. However, that definition is beyond the scope of what we need to cover here. Equity includes:

- Shareholder Investments (aka Contributions)
- Shareholder Draws (aka Distributions)
- Retained Earnings (aka Fuggedaboutit)

Are you hangin' in there? Good! It's time we head to our next stop in Accounting Land.

CHAPTER 5.
ADVANCED ACCOUNTING

Now that we've got the basics covered, it's time to do some advanced number crunching.

This is the kind of stuff that will help you understand what it costs you to do business. In addition, it will help you figure out whether you're operating at a loss or generating a profit. (Let's hope for the latter versus the former). Along the way I'll offer suggestions for putting those results to good use. Some of this material may strike you as awful to begin with, but stick with me. I'll make it as easy as I can.

These are the sorts of things we'll be talking about:

- Chart of Accounts (COA)
- Cost of Goods Sold (COGS)
- Profit & Loss (P&L) Statements
- Statement of Financial Position/Balance Sheets (BSs)

I know you can master these. When you do, you'll feel—and sound—like a seasoned expert.

Chart of Accounts

Your transactions are now organized into accounts. But how and where do the accounts themselves get organized? Well, that's easy. In your bookkeeping system, you'll find a master list of all of your accounts. It's called the Chart of Accounts. (Yes, it's that basic.) Sometimes it's referred to as a COA. We discussed account types earlier, in Chapter 4. We'll go over them, in greater detail, in a jiffy. For now, stick with me.

It's best to follow along with your accounting file open, so you can see what I'm talking about.

You'll need to be familiar with your COA going forward, so don't be afraid to really dig in. I've outlined three levels of accounts for you in a sample chart which appears later in this chapter. As you read from left to right, the accounts descend from greatest to least amount of detail. The far left column shows the account you'll be placing your transactions into. The third column is the Major Bucket it falls under.

Let's call these "Major-Level," "Mid-Level Description" and "Detail-Level" account categories. I'm sure there are more professional terms for these, but I'm not going to use them. The important thing is that you understand the general concept. Take a quick look at the COA in this chapter. Skim through the accounts at each level to get familiar with this idea. Then continue reading for further clarification.

Major-Level Accounts

We discussed the (5) Major-Level Accounts earlier. These appear in the third column, "Account Type:"

- Asset
- Expense
- Liability
- Revenue
- Equity

Mid-Level Description Accounts

The second column is where you'll find Mid-Level Description Accounts, under the heading "Account Description." Simple, right? The Mid-Level is where smaller, more specific buckets are housed. They describe the various types of transactions found within your Major-Level Accounts and allow for detail to be added to your reporting, so that you can get as specific as possible with your account information.

If you refer back to Chapter 4, you will see these Mid-Level Accounts described as sub-categories of the Major-Level Accounts. Because seeing it is easier than reading it, I don't describe every possible Mid-Level Account. In addition, it would be impossible to describe every potential scenario. So, I will avoid trying. We'll touch on the highlights and disregard anything that's self-explanatory.

Standard Mid-Level Account jargon you might use in everyday business conversation is outlined here (by corresponding Major-Level category) and includes:

Asset

- Accounts Receivable (A/R) – Money customers owe you
- Inventory – Product kept on-hand for selling to customers
- Current Assets – Assets which will convert to cash within 1 year
- Long-Term Assets – Assets which will be held longer than 1 year

Expense

- Cost of Goods Sold – Cost of material, labor and inventory to produce sales/deliver service
- Operating Expense (aka General & Administrative Expense) – Costs incurred to do business

Liability

- Accounts Payable (A/P) – Money you owe your vendors

- Current Liabilities – Lines of credit, credit cards and debts due within 1 year
- Long-Term Liabilities – Loans and debts with due dates of longer than 1 year

Revenue

- Sales of Product Income – Revenue earned from selling a product
- Service/Fee Income – Revenue earned from selling a service

Equity

- Owner's Draw – Money the owner takes out of the company
- Owner's Contribution – Money the owner contributes to the company

Detail-Level Accounts

The first column is where you'll find Detail-Level information, under the heading "Account Name." These are accounts you get to set up according to your specific business needs, though some Detail-Level Accounts may already be in place. This is dependent on your choice of accounting software. What appears in the example COA included in this chapter are standard types of Detail-Level entries.

You may find that you have a need for additional Detail-Level Accounts which aren't on that list, just as you may not have a use for some of the standard accounts you see mentioned. At this level, account names can and should be customized, or tailored, to suit your own company's requirements. When deciding to add a new Detail-Level Account to the mix, it helps to follow a few foolproof guidelines.

When Adding a Detail-Level Account

- Decide which Major Account category it falls under (i.e., Asset, Expense).
- Nest it under the Mid-Level Account best suited to it (i.e., A/R, COGS).
- Name your new Detail-Level Account so that it's descriptive and clear.

Bam! You've just created a new account. While the layout and rules which govern your COA are out of your control, the names you assign to these small bucket accounts are yours to mostly go crazy with. Still, keep in mind that everyone who's required to access or update this information on your behalf is privy to this labeling system. Name your accounts in a way that's intuitive and easily understood by all.

EXAMPLE: Chart of Accounts (COA)

Account List			
Account Name	**Account Description**	**Account Type**	**Description**
Business Checking	Bank	Asset	Checking Account
Business Savings	Bank	Asset	Savings Account
Cash on hand	Bank	Asset	Petty Cash On Hand
Accounts Receivable	Accounts receivable (A/R)	Asset	Amount due from customers
Inventory Asset	Other Current Assets	Asset	On-Hand inventory for sale
Accounts Payable	Accounts payable (A/P)	Liability	Amount due to vendors
Credit Card	Credit Card	Liability	Credit Card
Opening Balance Equity	Opening Balance Equity	Equity	System-used account for beginning bank balances
Owner's Contributions	Owner's Equity	Equity	Contributions from owner(s)
Owner's Draws	Owner's Equity	Equity	Draws from owner(s)
Retained Earnings	Retained Earnings	Equity	System-used account for earnings retained by company
Sales	Sales of Product Income	Revenue	Revenue earned from sales of product
Services	Service/Fee Income	Revenue	Revenue earned from services rendered
Cost of Goods Sold	Cost of Goods Sold	Expense	A direct cost of selling product or service
Advertising	Operating Expense	Expense	Advertising Expense
Bank Charges	Operating Expense	Expense	Bank Charges Expense
Charitable Contributions	Operating Expense	Expense	Charitable Contributions Expense
Computer Expense	Operating Expense	Expense	Computer Expense
Dues & Subscriptions	Operating Expense	Expense	Dues & Subscriptions Expense
Insurance	Operating Expense	Expense	Insurance Expense
Legal & Professional Fees	Operating Expense	Expense	Legal & Professional Fees Expense
Meals and Entertainment	Operating Expense	Expense	Meals and Entertainment Expense
Office Expense	Operating Expense	Expense	Office Expense
Postage And Delivery	Operating Expense	Expense	Postage And Delivery Expense
Rent or Lease	Operating Expense	Expense	Rent or Lease Expense
Payroll Expense	Operating Expense	Expense	Payroll Wages & Taxes
Repair & Maintenance	Operating Expense	Expense	Repair & Maintenance Expense
Research & Development	Operating Expense	Expense	Research & Development Expense
Software	Operating Expense	Expense	Software Expense
Subcontractors	Operating Expense	Expense	Subcontractors Expense
Taxes & Licenses	Operating Expense	Expense	Taxes & Licenses Expense
Travel	Operating Expense	Expense	Travel Expense
Utilities	Operating Expense	Expense	Utilities Expense
Website Expense	Operating Expense	Expense	Website Expense
Interest Earned	Operating Expense	Other Income	Interest Earned
Interest Expense	Operating Expense	Other Expense	Interest Expense

Ahhh, take a breather. You now know how to navigate your COA and speak the language. So far, so good. Let's recap what we've accomplished so far:

- You've learned what financials are good for and why keeping books is important.
- You discovered the many methods of keeping your books electronically.
- You've gotten a taste for the lingo and can now converse like a pro.
- You've categorized your transactions like a seasoned vet.
- Nothing can hold you back now — congratulations!

Let's move on to what happens to your data after your transactions are properly categorized.

Reports

Once you've organized all of your transactions into their proper buckets, what do you do next?

You've used your accounting software to categorize each of your transactions, but what do you do with the bucket totals? You run reports, of course! The benefit to all of this is being able to generate understandable summaries of information. The two most critical reports you will ever run are Income Statements and Balance Sheets, which provide a glimpse at the overall the health of your business.

Income Statement

Let's start with the bottom line. The grand finale. The pièce de résistance. Profit! That's your Income Statement. It's also called the Profit & Loss Statement. This is the go-to report you will always hear about. Get to know this one well. This is the primary report bankers, investors, CPAs and savvy business advisors will want to see, when it comes right down to taking the pulse of your business's financial status.

In the big picture view, this report accounts for all of the money you made, subtracts all of the money you spent and then tells you what's left over. If you made more than you spent, your business is profitable. If you spent more than you earned, you are operating at a loss. See the example provided here. Make special note of where the "Loss" or "Profit" number is located. This is the infamous "Bottom Line."

EXAMPLE: Profit & Loss (aka Income) Statement – Widget World, Inc.

Profit and Loss Statement
Widget World Inc.
Period Ending December 31, 20xx

Income	Amount
Product Sales	$74,500.00
Services Revenue	$4,900.00
Total Income	**$79,400.00**

Cost of Goods Sold

Cost of Goods Sold - Inventory	28,000.00
Cost of Goods Sold - Job Materials	4,500.00
Total Cost of Sales	**$32,500.00**

Gross Profit	**$46,900.00**

*Total Income less Cost of Goods Sold

Expenses

Advertising	2,250.00
Bank Charges	45.00
Computer Expenses	399.00
Dues & Subscriptions	466.78
Insurance	2,220.00
Meals & Entertainment	1,119.74
Office Expenses	830.26
Postage & Delivery	114.89
Taxes & Licenses	5,560.00
Travel Expenses	9,857.96
Wages & Payroll Expenses	17,734.09
Total Expenses	**$40,597.72**

Net Profit	**$6,302.28**

*Gross Profit less Expenses

Balance Sheet

The second, standard financial report we will discuss is the Balance Sheet. This report is also referred to as a Statement of Financial Position. Generating this report reveals what the ending balances are of your Asset, Liability and Equity accounts over a given period of time. They are usually set to run along parameters which help you aggregate a month's, a quarter's or a whole year's worth of data.

This report takes a snapshot of the balances for each account and puts them in the form of a report. It is helpful to review at month's end, letting you know how much money remains in your checking account, what balances you carry on your credit accounts and what remains outstanding on loans due. It will also outline your owner contributions to the business year-to-date (YTD).

Banks like to see Balance Sheets. They often run ratios and do analyses on these numbers to see if you have enough cash and assets to cover your bills. This report also helps you keep track of investors' equity balances. Say you gave an investor equity in exchange for capital they provided, which was supplied to you in the form of money or other valuable assets. That equity would then appear on your Balance Sheet.

EXAMPLE: Balance Sheet (aka Statement of Financial Position) – Widget World, Inc.

Balance Sheet
Widget World Inc.
Period Ending December 31, 2xxx

Assets			
Current Assets			
	Cash On Hand	$44.75	
	Checking Account	$1,255.98	
	Savings Account	$800.00	
	Accounts Receivable	$1,800.00	
	Total Current Assets	**$3,900.73**	
Fixed Assets			
	Fixed Assets - Equipment	$22,000.00	
	Building & Land	$75,000.00	
	Total Fixed Assets	**$97,000.00**	
Inventory			
	Inventory On Hand	$23,608.00	
	Total Inventory	**$23,608.00**	
Total Assets			**$124,508.73**
Liabilities			
Current Liabilities			
	Credit Card	$433.65	
	Accounts Payable	$722.80	
	Total Current Liabilities	**$1,156.45**	
Long Term Liabilities			
	Bank Loan	$20,000.00	
	Building & Land Loan Due	$75,000.00	
	Total Long Term Liabilities	**$95,000.00**	
Total Liabilities			**$96,156.45**
Net Assets (Assets less Liabilities)			**$28,352.28**
Equity			
Equity	Owner's Contributions	$35,000.00	
	Less Owner's Draws	$12,950.00	
	Retained Earnings	$6,302.28	
Total Equity			**$28,352.28**

*Net Assets should equal Total Equity

Yes, there are loads of other reports you can run.

There are also various other ways to analyze the buckets of money you own or manage. Still, these are two you absolutely need to know about. You might say they're the Matterhorns and Cyclones of Accounting Land. Adventures you simply must experience at least once in your lifetime. Or, when it comes to business, once a year. Once a quarter. Preferably? Once a month!

Stop! Run Away

Since we're on the topic of Advanced Accounting, I'll share some questionable data with you.

I deliberated over whether to include it. In the end, I was told it'd be great bonus material for anyone who's taken a shine to this accounting stuff. That said, if your eyes start crossing and your head starts hurting, feel free to stop reading and run the other way. Debit, Credit and Double-Entry Accounting are topics which aren't exactly pertinent to this discussion, but they are (apparently) quite tantalizing.

Debit & Credit

I warn you now that neither of those terms means what you think it means. For the most part, the only time people hear the words debit and credit is at a bank. That is NOT what you should think about, in this context. When you make a deposit, the teller says she will "credit your account." When you return something to the store, you hear you're getting store "credit."

Those phrases are accurate in (2) ways:

- They are both accounting terms.
- They indeed refer to a type of adjustment being made on your account.

The problem with this terminology is that it's used with *their* perspective in mind—either the teller's or the store clerk's. The takeaway here is, as you manage your books, you must ignore those definitions altogether. They simply don't pertain to you. What they describe is what's happening to affect the bank or the store itself. It would be like describing your books from your vendor's viewpoint. A waste of time.

Debit and credit are, however, related to Double Entry Accounting. That's what we'll close out with.

Double Entry Accounting

For those who like to get a good look at the big picture, there's Double Entry Accounting. Each transaction you carry out affects two or more accounts within your books. That's why this process is thusly named. Here's an example: When you pay an insurance bill, you put that expense into the "Insurance Expense" bucket o' money and take it out of the "Checking Account" bucket. Thus, two accounts are affected.

BELOW: A cheater's diagram for handling Debits and Credits.

We know that each transaction affects two or more accounts. It affects them, incidentally, with at least one debit and one credit. Here, "debit" and "credit" are used to refer to the opposite sides of the accounting entry and not the plus or minus (+/-) your bank attaches to it. The running balance of each account is affected in a unique way by either a debit or a credit. I've outlined them below:

Debit & Credit Effect on the (5) Major Accounts

	DEBIT	**CREDIT**
Assets	Increase	*Decrease*
Expenses	Increase	*Decrease*
Liabilities	*Decrease*	Increase
Revenues	*Decrease*	Increase
Equity	*Decrease*	Increase

Take another look at the cheater's diagram. Now, let's walk through payment of that insurance bill.

When you pay that bill, you effectively increase the amount you've thrown into your "Insurance Expense" bucket. This creates a debit. A necessary second step, per Double-Entry Accounting rules, is to ensure that those funds are also accounted for in your "Assets" bucket, which you drew from to cover the expense. That's because, in real life, you use assets from your bank account to pay your insurance bill.

Put even more plainly, when you pay that bill your expenses increase (via a debit) and your assets decrease (via a credit). The entire transaction winds up looking like this:

	DEBIT	CREDIT
Insurance Expense	$100.00	
Cash (to cover it)		$100.00

Remember that, as the rules of the Double Entry Accounting game go, there must be two entries per transaction—and the two must equal one another, cancelling each other out.

CHAPTER 6. GETTING DOWN TO BRASS TACKS
(Finally, You Get to Do Your Books!)

How's your trip through Accounting Land so far? It's not really all that bad, is it?

I think you'll like it even more once we get down to brass tacks and tackle what it is you're here to do. Your bookkeeping! Regardless of which financial software program you use, the ten steps I've outlined below remain the same. That's great news, right? I'm about to walk you through this section, which is further broken down by: What You'll Need, Where You'll Find It and What You'll Do Next.

Are you ready to do some bookkeeping? (I like your attitude!) Let's get 'er done.

What You'll Need

- Accounting software
- Bank login information
- A decision: Cash or Accrual?
- Receipts for non-business account transactions

- *Optional:* Caffeine and soothing background music

Where You'll Find It

Consider Steps 1 thru 6, which immediately follow, your "prep" work. The good news is, you've already done or learned how to do a few of these things. So, take relief in knowing that, in order to get your bookkeeping done right, you won't have to work nearly as hard as you once thought. Imagine that!

Step 1: *Get familiar with your accounting software.*

If you still need help choosing an accounting software system, revisit Chapter 3. Then open that puppy up and poke around. Don't be shy! Help menus should be available to assist you. There are also plenty of tutorials available on YouTube. Perhaps you know someone who can teach you to use your software. Do a combination of all of these, learning how your program operates.

Step 2: *Properly set up your Chart of Accounts.*

Most accounting systems allow you to add new accounts to your COA at will, so this step can be done as we move forward. That'll both save time and prevent you from adding account types you may not ever need. If you want to get really creative, most bookkeeping software systems allow you to create sub-accounts. This leads to even better organization of your bookkeeping records.

For example, let's say you want to create sub-accounts under the "Travel" category so you can capture and isolate "Transportation" and "Travel Meal" expenses. That's a great way to make viewing your reports easier and to group like items. We'll explore more of that later. For now, I recommend that you start by setting up "Bank" and "Credit Card" accounts. You'll need them!

Step 3: *Decide on either the Cash or Accrual method.*

From here on out, I will assume that you have decided to manage your books on a Cash basis. If you chose Accrual, you'll still be able to follow along. Keep in mind, however, that we won't be addressing ways you can make note of Accounts Payable (i.e., vendor bills due) or Accounts Receivable (i.e., customer invoices due) data using that specific method.

Step 4: *Set up and connect Bank Feeds via your accounting software.*

Take advantage of your software system's Bank Feeds option. This should be simple to do, since most accounting programs walk you through each step. Bank feeds link your software to your bank account(s), saving you the hassle of manually downloading transactions. This is especially helpful long-term, since most banks only display 90 days' worth of transactions at a time.

Step 5: *One at a time, log into your bank accounts.*

When logging into each account, this is what you'll look for and then do:

- *Bank Statements* – Pull up one statement for each month you plan to cover in this bookkeeping session, saving a copy of each to your computer. You'll use these to reconcile each account you own. To "reconcile the bank" means to match up your ending bank statement balance to your ending accounting software balance. By double-checking these numbers, you ensure that all transactions are accounted for.

- *Bank Transactions* – If you've set up a Bank Feed (Step 4), you may not have to download any bank transactions at all. Your software will have done it for you! Still, check to see whether it's imported transactions for the entire period you want to cover in this bookkeeping session. *If so,* no need to do what the software has already done: Skip

"Download Files" below. *If not,* complete "Download Files."

- *Download Files* – The online portals for most bank accounts feature a "My Account" tab or screen. That's where you'll find a link, which allows you to download any missing transactions. It may also be labeled "Export," "Download Transactions" or "Download Activity." Click on that link and enter the date range you still need information for. Choose the format, or file type, which corresponds to your software (.ofx, .csv, etc.). Save each of these files to your computer. Be sure to label them well. For example, YEAR-MO-BankName (2020-01-BanksRUs).

- *Business Accounts* – Repeat the steps above for every single bank or credit card account that's associated with your business. That means each one you plan to put in sync with and account for using your financial software program.

Step 6: *Locate your receipts. (Yep, all of them!)*

The IRS usually requires and often politely requests that you save all of your business transaction documentation. That's a great practice and a great reason to complete Step 5 above. Here, though, I'm not asking you to track down receipts for purchases made using your business bank accounts. You've downloaded that info. I'm talking about receipts for purchases you may have forgotten to account for:

- Receipts for cash purchases
- Receipts for business purchases (or, gasp, deposits!) from your personal accounts

The many places these receipts are commonly found hiding include:

- Your Wallet
- Your Desk Drawers
- Your Car's Glove Box
- Your Home's Kitchen Counter
- Under Stacks of Unfiled Paperwork

Worst case? Since these transactions were made in association with your personal bank or credit card accounts, records of them can be found by skimming through paper statements or your online transaction records with those institutions. Check each month's transactions for the period you'll be updating your financials for. Save copies of related statements to your computer.

What You'll Do Next

Things are starting to heat up. This is where we begin really digging into the task of bookkeeping. All of that preparation and earlier familiarization with the rules, guidelines and lingo of accounting will pay of hugely here. HUGELY, I say!

Step 7: *Upload the banking information you've gathered together.*

- Your accounting software provides an option to upload or import your transactions.

- Follow the steps to do this. (Each program is a little bit different.) At first, this may seem foreign. In my experience, accounting software generally makes this quite simple and is designed to guide you through the process step-by-step. If you're ever unsure of what to do next, explore the Help section or watch a YouTube video.
- Note: If you're using an Excel spreadsheet, your banking information was probably downloaded as a .csv file. You can either copy and paste that data into a new spreadsheet or

manipulate the data within the file you downloaded and rename it.

- Once the upload is complete, you should get an alert telling you that your data has successfully been imported into your accounting program.

- Repeat this process for each of your business accounts.

Step 8: *Review your bank transactions, looking for themes.*

It's time to review and categorize that data. Your accounting program now contains all of your imported transactions. They're just waiting for you, in what's sometimes called a Bank Feed or Uncoded Transaction list. This step will help you get them out of limbo, on the books and in the right buckets. You'll add vendors, assign them to accounts stored in your COA and voila!

- Navigate to the Bank Feed/Uncoded Transaction list.

- Identify each bank account you've added transactions for.

- Select a bank account or credit card account to work on first.
- As you complete these steps, take note of the options available to you.

- Next, sort the list. Do this however you prefer. TIP: I prefer to sort them by "Description" or "Memo," so I can work on like transactions simultaneously.

- Pick a place to start. The top of the list is sometimes the simplest place to begin.

- As needed or desired, assign a "Vendor" or "Customer" to each transaction. This allows you to view all related transactions in the Vendor/Customer portal at a later date. I advise it, since bank memos don't always transfer over with transaction data, leaving you no additional information to go by.

- Assign each transaction to the appropriate account, or bucket, in your COA. If the account you want to use isn't in your COA, add it from the Bank Feed/Uncoded Transaction list. If a particular transaction needs to be split up into two different accounts, there should be an option for that. For example, you purchase both a stapler for your office and an oil change for your company car at Walmart or Costco. They appear on the same receipt. You need to be able to split those individual transactions into the "Office Supply" and "Auto" buckets.

- When you're done adding Vendor/Customer and appropriate account information for a given transaction, click "Add" to get it officially on your books.

- Repeat this process until all transactions from each bank account are added.

I realize that sometimes categorizing transactions isn't as easy as it sounds. There may be times when picking an account turns into a philosophical debate. If in doubt, your accountant and even Google are good resources. The best advice I can give you is to be reasonable with your choices and to be consistent across all transactions of the same type, grouping like items together.

Step 9: *Trust in the process – but verify everything.*

Congratulations! That's probably the biggest chunk of work you'll do here.

While I want you to trust in yourself and your work, you must verify that everything's complete. I recommend reconciling the bank accounts appearing in your software to the bank statements you receive from your bank. (If you're a nerd like me, this will be fun.) Your accounting software records should mimic what happened in real life and not contain anything that didn't transpire.

In order to reconcile your accounts, you are going to literally match the transactions you added to your books with the transactions which posted to your bank statement. This ensures that your bookkeeping efforts account for every transaction. It also ensures that no additional transactions were added in error. (Transactions which were, say, personal vs. business-related.)

1. Locate the "Reconcile" option in your software menu.

2. Select the bank or credit account you want to reconcile.

3. Enter the ending date of the bank statement. TIP: Reconcile monthly. Aim to do that at the beginning of

each new month, when the bank has prepared your most recent bank statement.

4. Enter the ending bank balance and statement closing date, as they appear on the bank statement.

5. Work your way through the statement from beginning to end, verifying that all of the transactions match up. Some software programs have built-in check boxes you can use to mark off transactions as you compare them with your bank statement. Others attempt to automatically reconcile things for you.

6. If the balances don't match, review the transactions line-by-line.

7. If something appears on your bank statement but not on your books, investigate why it's missing. Correcting the issue may require you to manually enter the transaction into your accounting system bank register.

8. If something appears on your books but not on your bank

statement, investigate why it's there. Correcting the issue may require you to make a note of it, delete it from your accounting system bank register and ask your accountant to intervene.

9. REMEMBER: Your system records and your bank records must match up exactly.

10. Repeat this process for all accounts and for each month you're updating.

Step 10: *Find a way to back up your company's financials.*

If you're using a desktop accounting software program or another offline option, it is important to always create a backup copy of your bookkeeping records. That way, if your computer crashes, you'll have a copy saved on a disc or a jump drive. If you're using an online program, this may not be necessary or possible. Print copies or screenshots are great solutions and workarounds.

That's it. *Clap at all of your hard work!*

Did you have trouble posting a particular transaction? If so, your accounting software system should be equipped a "Clearing," "Suspense" or "Ask My Accountant" bucket. If not, create one. Move related items into this bucket and contact your accountant for advice on how to handle the situation. The next chapter deals with common trouble spots, so you may find answers there.

CHAPTER 7.
COMPLICATIONS
(Yep, Everyone Has 'Em!)

What's a trip to Accounting Land without a few twists and turns?

By now, you've done most of the real work involved in bookkeeping. You have a basic understanding of the rules of accounting and some idea of what you want to achieve with your financials. You no doubt also have concerns you aren't sure you're equipped to address. Perhaps there are expenses you can't categorize. Or maybe you've put personal funds into the business and don't know how to classify that.

This chapter addresses complications encountered by most businesses.

Keep in mind that some questions or situations are more complex than the scope of this book can provide answers for. We can't cover every situation because, well, this book would never end. My goal is to teach you the basics of bookkeeping and to help you organize your books quickly and easily—as this book's title suggests. Make note of your unanswered questions and then hire an accountant who can answer them.

As you move forward, feel free to skim the headings in search of what you're looking for.

Bank Loans (aka Liabilities)

When you get a loan from a bank, two things happen: 1.) You receive a cash deposit or certified check from that institution for the agreed-upon amount, and, 2.) You owe that bank a balance due on the loan. The most common error people make when making a loan payment is to treat this as an Expense, calling it something like "Loan Repayment." The reason this is tricky is because it's not an expense at all.

The money received is not considered Revenue, either. That's because it's not money earned but, rather, money that is now due to the bank or lender. The related deposit of funds actually creates a "Liability." A new account should be added to your COA, helping you track the loan.

Loan payments, then, simply reduce the amount you owe the bank in repayment for what it advanced you. If you look at your Balance Sheet, your bank loan should appear as a Liability. Each loan payment you make serves as a reduction of that liability and lowers the outstanding balance owed. If loan payments appear anywhere on your Profit & Loss (aka Revenue and Expense) report, you must re-categorize them.

Bank Interest

Interest is generated through your bank when your money is kept in an interest-earning account. Typical examples include Money Market and Savings accounts. With an interest-earning account, the bank periodically pays you interest. When this interest is received, it is a common error to lump it in with your normal income. However, it's not normal oncome.

This is an "Other Income" transaction and should be labeled, more specifically, "Interest Income." When you look at your P&L, you will notice that this section appears at the bottom of the report just above your Net Profit/Loss. Conversely, when the bank charges you interest on loans or lines of credit, this is considered an "Other Expense" and should be further identified as an "Interest Expense."

Transfers Between Accounts

Once upon a time I was hired by a company whose owner was fantastic at running his business.

He also tried really, really hard to keep good books and for the most part did a great job. Now I'll tell you how he inadvertently messed them up. This particular client had a credit card which he frequently used for business purposes. These business expenses appeared in his books and everything looked fine. When he paid his credit card bill, he intuitively created an Expense account called "Credit Card Payments."

This makes complete sense, right? Wrong.

Looking at his Balance Sheet, his credit card balance seemed way too high. It was also being reported incorrectly, as no payments were applied in the books. Even worse, he wound up accounting for expenses twice: as they happened (Deduction #1) and as he entered related payments into his credit card payment bucket (Deduction #2). While this is a big problem for the taxman, it also really messes up your P&L.

By noting twice the expense, your profits are reported as being twice as low! The moral of this story? When you move money from one business account to another, it is considered a "Transfer." This includes using money in a checking account to pay a credit card bill. Think of it as shifting money from one account to another. It does not and should not affect your Income or Expenses one little bit.

Investments in the Business

There are generally two types of investments made in your business: Money contributed by the owner and money invested by partners. The latter is often called Partnership Equity. We'll discuss both here.

Owner Investments

When you started your company, you probably sunk a bunch of your own money into it. After all, it takes money to build an empire and that money needs to come from somewhere! When you put money into your business, it can be treated in one of two ways. You can either consider it a loan or a contribution. What differs is whether you intend to be paid back or not. If you want your money back, it's a loan (or Liability). If you want it to remain in the business, as an investment, it's an Owner Contribution (Equity).

Partner Investments

When other people (such as business partners) invest money in your company, those funds fall under the category of Equity. No, we will not get into stocks or partnerships here. Those topics are too far-reaching and advanced for this book. Just know that, if people contribute things of value to your company, their investments get placed in an Equity bucket of their own — which must be tracked and accounted for.

Draws/Paychecks (aka Getting Paid)

Draw or paycheck? Ask your tax professional which you should do, as the business owner.

Certain types of business formations (i.e., Corporations) require the owner to take a paycheck with appropriate taxes deducted from it. Others types of business formations (i.e., Sole Proprietorships) require the owner to take a draw. Find out from your tax professional which type of compensation you should be taking, as the business owner.

An Owner Draw, or distribution, is the opposite of an Owner Contribution. In its most basic definition, it involves removing money from the company. This type of "paycheck" isn't really a paycheck. No taxes are deducted at the time of distribution. Instead, taxes are paid at the end of the year or quarterly, in line with requirements or standards set by the IRS. This puts you in the role of a contractor versus employee.

If you are advised to take payment as an employee, it is preferable to use a payroll processing system or service. Calculating taxes is intense work and most service fees are extremely reasonable considering the headaches they prevent. Within the payroll system, you would be set up as a regular employee. Taxes would be withheld from each of your paychecks and submitted to the government on your behalf, as if you were working anywhere else.

Comingling of Business & Personal Funds

Spending personal funds on business expenses is hard to avoid. Yet, spending business funds on personal expenses should be avoided at all costs. This situation is called "comingling of funds" and it can easily backfire since it is often tricky to account for. Comingling should always be avoided. That said, if you need to account for transactions which happened previously, here's how you can deal with it:

Business Funds for Personal Use

If you spent company money on personal expenses, there are two ways you can classify them. The first is to create an account under "Other Expense" that is called "Personal Expenses" and categorize them there. The second is to simply categorize these transactions under "Owner Draw" or distribution. Note, however, that the Personal Expense method will affect your P&L bottom line. Decide which is best for you. (I prefer the distribution method.)

Personal Funds Used for Business Expenses

> If you paid for Business Expenses using personal funds, there are two ways to classify those, as well. (We actually touched on this earlier.) First, decide whether you want the business to reimburse you or not. If so, consider the funds a loan to your company and create an account under "Liability" that is called something like "Due to Owner." If not, simply categorize these transactions under "Owner Contributions" in the larger Equity bucket.

I bet you're thinking, "Crystal, this doesn't make any sense! My personal accounts aren't linked to my software. How do I get these transactions entered onto my books?" The answer is through the use of a Journal Entry. Like Double Entry Accounting, journal entries are complex business. Still, I'm confident you'll find a number of tutorials online which explain exactly how you might put them to good use.

Refunds

Refunds are common in everyday life. You buy something, decide you don't want it and return it to the brick and mortar (or online) store you bought it from. You then get your money back. But where does that money go? That's easy! You categorize the reversal in the same Expense account you put the original purchase in. This cancels out the first transaction and corrects the running tally of your Expense bucket.

Yet, since it's often processed as a bank credit, a common mistake is to classify this as "Income."

With refunds, always aim to reflect reality. While your refund may appear as a bank credit or deposit, this is misleading. It doesn't qualify as income, because you didn't earn it in the course of business. Conversely, categorizing it in the Expense account it originated with lets you "undo" the purchase. If you *neglect* to cancel out that original expense, your Expenses will appear higher than they actually were.

Other Revenue

This was touched on earlier. Because it's important, it's worth repeating.

If you've received money from any of the following sources, it will be considered "Other Income." If you refer back to the sample COA, this information falls near the bottom next to "Other Expenses." It is wise to get expert assistance with some of these. That's because they need to be reported in a way that shows lenders, tax professionals and government agencies where your funds came from.

Other Revenue Sources

- Insurance Payouts
- Bank-Issued Interest
- Money Found on the Street
- Bank or Credit Line Advances
- Crowdsourcing Campaign Funds
- Money Gained in a Lawsuit Settlement

Also lumped in here are any funds received from sources other than customers. These types of deposits are highly unusual and rarely occur. When they do and are not categorized as "Other Revenue," they are usually classified as Liabilities.

Let's say your business owns the building it's in and you decide to rent out an otherwise empty office to a tenant, who gives you a deposit. Technically speaking, if they're nice to you and live up to all of their contractual obligations, you owe that money back to them at the end of their lease term should they choose to vacate. The deposit they paid is not considered "Other Revenue."

What it amounts to is a bank deposit, representing money you owe someone else—the tenant—which is super weird to think about, I know! All of these things show up in your financial reports as money received but NOT in the course of doing business as usual.

Other Expenses

"Other Expenses" are a lot like "Other Revenue," except that you pay these rather than receive them.

Other Expenses

- Interest Expenses
- Fraudulent Charges
- Lawsuit Settlement Payouts
- Money That Fell Out of Your Pocket

These are often expenses your business bore but which are unrelated to your core business operations. For example, say you pay interest on a credit card bill. Interest payments are unrelated to the core function of your business. You may argue that it's a "Business Expense"—a fee on a line of credit you used to buy materials to keep things running, etc. That's a philosophical debate I do not want to enter into.

Core business expenses include things like employee wages, electricity and production materials.

Employees vs. Contractors

Employee vs. Contractor is a conundrum as old as time. One nearly everyone experiences confusion over. We'll discuss the basic differences, so you know how to classify the people who do work for you.

Employee

Someone whose job duties are dictated by you. The tools and supplies they use are provided by you. They are given the benefits of pension plans, holiday pay and/or insurance packages, in exchange for continued employment. You put employees on payroll and withhold the appropriate payroll taxes from their checks.

Contractor

Someone who dictates their own hours and sets guidelines related to any assistance they provide you with. They bring their own tools and supplies to the job. They receive no fringe benefits from you. They procure and pay for their own insurance plans. You simply write them a check for payment in full or incrementally, as outlined in terms you jointly agree to and per the invoice they supply you with.

Please note that these are general definitions and that they are in no way exhaustive. There are certainly exceptions to every rule and there is not a single answer to any one of your questions. When in doubt, call a trusted accountant or lawyer for information and assistance.

CHAPTER 8. WHY BOTHER?
(Staying on Top of Your Books Is a Good Thing)

Savvy business owners know one thing for sure: Their numbers matter.

They strive to have current books at all times. This helps them identify trends and stay on budget. It makes tax filing easier, eliminating the need for a Finance degree. It intrigues investors and satisfies tax collectors. It makes running a business easier overall. You, too, now have a vast understanding of your finances, know how your books should function and can pull a few snazzy moves with little to no help.

Now's the time to look ahead—because staying on top of your books matters, too!

Keep Growing

Some business owners believe that, if there's money in the bank, they are doing well. This is only partially true. The other side to that truth is that there's a very good chance much of that money doesn't belong to you. Taxes, vendors, employees and landlords all need to be paid. You're just the temporary guardian, or holder, of that money. Sooner or later you'll have to do something with it.

Bookkeeping comes in handy by helping you keep track of all the debts you owe, all the debts which are owed to you and any bills you need to pay to keep things running smoothly. As you update your books, you gain insight into growth trends and get a peek at what's lagging behind. You can then make a plan that's well suited to either situation. For example, is your business growing or stagnant?

Can you afford to order more inventory, taking advantage of a volume discount? Is there money enough to hire another employee who can help grow your business, by responding to and filling a backlog of customer requests? With the numbers in front of you, what do you project your budget will be for the coming year? Based on that information, is it possible to increase your Owner's Draw?

Reading and staying on top of your financials enables you to keep growing, in the right direction.

Know Your Numbers

When you speak to an investor who truly knows what he or she is doing, the first thing they'll ask after you wrap up your pitch is: "What are your numbers?" If you don't know, you should. (In that instance, you'll wish you did.) While perhaps wrongly accused of being dull, your financials beat in time with the heart of your business. Scratch that. They are the heart of your business, be it healthy or struggling.

If you've decided to outsource this task, communicate regularly with your bookkeeper.

He or she is your direct line to higher profits and should act as one of your primary, trusted advisors. Just as you have a hand in daily operations and are keyed in to all of the other important aspects of your business, fiscal oversight is your responsibility. Less "free handing" of your money can occur if you remain actively involved on the financial side and remain aware of who's been paid and who's paying you.

Think, "Money's Sexy!"

I'm not about to say that doing your bookkeeping is sexy — but making money is. So, even if you consider the task of bookkeeping on par with going to the dentist, remember that it's hard for anyone to resist the allure of a bright, shiny smile. Fun or not, doing the books and then wisely investing in your business growth will up your potential for success and earnings like nobody's business. (And that's definitely sexy!)

Avoid Tax Time Panic

As April 15th looms on the horizon, Tax Time Panic sinks in. This is a race that gets old really quickly. At the start of each year, a daunting feeling overcomes the masses: "Oh, great! Taxes are due." Is that what you call a good time? Me either. Make a plan to get organized and stick with it each and every month. Make your books an obsession, imagining you're Scrooge McDuck. Count your piles of cash, put them in the appropriate buckets and watch them grow. You'll be thankful come April. I all but guarantee it!

CHAPTER 9.
PULLING IT TOGETHER FOR YOUR CPA

The tax man will want a lot of information from you, in order to calculate your tax bill.

First and foremost, that information should account for any deductions and credits you claim. It should also outline what your business spent on operating costs. During an audit, you'll need to present copies of your financial reports which substantiate amounts you've previously claimed. This sort of information can be found in the "Reports" section of your accounting program, which will help you compile every bit of it.

Reports and records which will help a Certified Public Accountant, or CPA, prepare you for a tax filing – or an audit – include:

- Trial Balances
- Balance Sheets
- General Ledgers
- Profit & Loss Statements
- Employee Pay Summaries
- Tax Forms Received (i.e., from clients/customers)

While we won't discuss most of these in detail here, your CPA will request related financial records, documentation and reports. That's because his or her primary goal is to gain thorough knowledge of your business finances. This allows them to assist you in staying one step ahead of the tax man, by submitting accurate information to the IRS while filing taxes on your behalf.

Reports and financial records commonly requested by CPAs include:

- Receipts
- Mileage Logs
- Fixed Assets Lists
- Bank Statements
- Bank Interest Statements
- Income Statement Reports
- Balance Sheets

If you really want to flaunt your newfound bookkeeping and accounting knowledge, collect up this info in advance and send it to your CPA before you meet to go over things in detail.

Receipts

Believe it or not, even in the digital age some form of receipt is crucial.

Receipts offer proof of purchase and are used to substantiate business expenses. As is also the case with Mileage Logs, you should be able to produce documentation which reveals a few specific things about each business expense you claim, in connection with a deduction, when filing. For receipts, those include:

- Date
- Amount
- Seller/Vendor
- Business Purpose
- Client Name (ex: Travel, Meal, Gift or Entertainment-related expenses)

If you're the subject of an IRS audit and can't show receipts for your purchases, you could be denied those deductions. This, of course, would be a less than desirable scenario.

Mileage Log

Mileage Logs are needed in a wide variety of circumstances.

It is best to always keep one, regardless of which vehicle you may be driving. This is true even if you choose to deduct actual vehicle costs rather than to account for miles driven. If you prefer the tech route, there are apps available which can help you with this. Information you generally need to include is:

- Date
- Start Mileage
- Ending Mileage
- Business Purpose
- Client Names (if applicable)

Even if you use a dedicated company truck or vehicle, it is best to keep a log that verifies everything you've reported. This comes in handy when auditors begin asking questions about documentation. Visit my website, CrystalWambeke.com, to download your FREE copy of the mileage log which appears here.

EXAMPLE: Mileage Log

Date	Destination	Business Purpose	Starting Mileage	Ending Mileage	Total Miles
			TOTAL MILES		

Fixed Assets (aka Capital Assets)

We mentioned Fixed Assets, or Capital Assets, earlier. They typically include vehicles, buildings, equipment, land, computers, other hardware and software. Normal practice is to set a threshold to determine what should be considered a fixed asset. You can determine this limit for yourself. A common threshold for small businesses is $500. For larger businesses, $5,000 is generally considered appropriate.

By the way, the dollar limit you set to determine assets is called a Capitalization Threshold. *(Bam!)*

These sorts of assets are owned by the business and have a useful life longer than one reporting period, which is normally one year. They might be patents, buildings, heavy machinery and furniture. Not all items you own are required to be categorized as fixed or capital assets. For example, it is uncommon to categorize any asset which is low in cost or has a useful life of less than two years.

Work with your CPA to determine the best approach for your business. Be sure to also keep good records for large purchases you make throughout the year. This will help the CPA assist you in making an informed determination. When you purchase a capital asset, assign it its own Asset account named after the item purchased. As a result, the item is then said to be "capitalized." *(More fancy jargon for you!)*

Rock Those Financials

Without further ado, I'd like to say, "Congratulations."

You are now master of your own Bookkeeping Kingdom. You've gone from novice to expert and it all happened without too much crying. (That's my hope!) You have words like "capitalization threshold" to throw around at parties. You know your Liability balances and can proudly show them off at partner meetings. You can even impress your CPA, who will marvel at your high level of organization.

I'm proud of all you've achieved. Now, go forth and continue to rock those financials!

APPENDIX

What good is a resource book without resources? This isn't an exhaustive list, but it's a good starting point. I also suggest searching online for video tutorials related to your accounting software program.

Bookkeeping

Crystal Wambeke
Owner of Crystal Wambeke, LLC
Accountant & Certified Bookkeeper
Crystal@CrystalWambeke.com
Office: (844) 227-9782
CrystalWambeke.com

Government

Internal Revenue Service
IRS.gov

Small Business Administration
SBA.gov

SCORE Association
SCORE.org

U.S. Department of the Treasury
Treasury.gov

Accounting Software

Fresh Books
FreshBooks.com

Mint
Mint.com

Wave Apps
WaveApps.com

QuickBooks
Intuit.com

Xero
Xero.com

General, Accounting & Finance

Investopedia
Investopedia.com

National Society of Accountants
NSAcct.org

GLOSSARY

Cash vs. Accrual

- Cash – Transactions are recorded on the date money changes hands.
- Accrual – Transactions are recorded upon origination and are tracked as either "Accounts Receivable" or "Accounts Payable" items until their status is resolved.

Transaction
The word used to describe the act of buying or selling goods or services.

Financial Records
Formal documents that are used to outline collective business transactions

Accounting Database
A system used to collect, store and process financial records

Revenue
Money Earned in the normal course of business

Expenditure
Money spent in the course of business

Asset
Cash or cash equivalent owned by the business

Current Assets
Assets that will convert to cash within 1 year

Long-Term Assets
Assets that will be held longer than 1 year

Liability
Debt owed by the business

Equity
Funding or assets contributed by shareholders

Chart of Accounts
The list of all accounts used in an accounting database

Cost of Goods Sold (COGS)
Cost of material, labor and inventory to produce sales/deliver service

Accounts Receivable (A/R)
Money customers owe you

Inventory
Product kept on-hand for selling to customers

Operating Expense (aka General & Administrative Expense)
Costs incurred to do business

Accounts Payable (A/P)
Money you owe your vendors

Current Liabilities
Lines of credit, credit cards and debts due within 1 year

Long-Term Liabilities
Loans and debts with due dates of longer than 1 year

Sales of Product Income
Revenue earned from selling a product

Service/Fee Income
Revenue earned from selling a service

Owner's Draw
Money the owner takes out of the company

Owner's Contribution
Money the owner contributes to the company

Fixed Assets (aka Capital Assets)
Assets purchased for long-term use; not probable to be converted to cash or sold

Profit & Loss (P&L) Statements
A summary report of all revenue, COGS, and expenses for a specified period of time

Statement of Financial Position/Balance Sheets (BSs)
A summary report of all asset, liability, and equity account balances as of a specified date

ACKNOWLEDGEMENTS

First and foremost, I'd like to thank my husband Michael. He is tirelessly supportive, always has the ability to make me laugh, applauds my nerdy tendencies and thinks I can move the Earth. I love you like crazy. And our dog, Jack, who always keeps my feet warm while I write.

Second, I'd like to thank my parents. Dad, you showed me that hard work pays off, that being kind matters and that it's important to enjoy the journey. Mom, thanks for *always* believing in me, showing me what bravery looks like, having the best advice (and laugh!), picking up the phone, being my rock and being twice as amazing as I could ever hope to be. Skip, thanks for encouraging me to challenge myself, work hard and appreciate the little things. I love you all.

I also want to recognize other friends and family members who demonstrate support for each of my crazy adventures. I wouldn't trade you for anything. This list is short and likely incomplete. I apologize now, if I forgot to mention anyone by name: Bob, Linda, Amanda, Josh, Dustin, Jill, Kari, Jaymason, Alesia, Dani, Travis N., Robin and everyone else. I love y'all!

Very special thanks go out to, first, Mr. Pickering—for being the best Accounting teacher and for taking pity on me ... when I still didn't understand the homework assignment, though it may have been 8:05 a.m. on the day it was due, even if that meant it was the last day of school. I'll never forget your goodwill! (←See what I did there? ☺ It's an accounting joke, folks!)

And second, Mr. Sogge, for teaching me about grammar and writing. Most of all, however, for reinforcing that to have integrity is a good thing. They say one person can't make a difference. You're proof that they can.

Last but not least, Cathy. You were the best boss ever and are now a great friend. Thanks for showing me the ropes, for teaching me what patience looks like and for always being so inspiring.

ABOUT the AUTHOR

Crystal Wambeke is a Certified Bookkeeper recognized by the American Institute of Professional Bookkeepers. Her penchant for providing meticulous, accurate accounting and bookkeeping services has benefited small and mid-sized organizations across the U.S. since 2007.

As Principal Accountant at Crystal Wambeke, LLC, she educates, trains and advises business leaders on topics ranging from Expense Management and Financial Projection to Managerial Finance. She presents before organizations, has served on several boards of directors and has developed Bookkeeping curricula used in small business centers housed within American colleges and universities.

In addition, Crystal actively advocates for and supports military, military spouse and women-owned businesses. In 2015, she received an "Outstanding Leadership Award" from the EBV-F program run by the Institute for Veteran and Military Families at Syracuse University.

A Minnesota native, she currently resides in North Carolina with her husband and their energetic dog. In her downtime, Crystal is an avid foodie, travel enthusiast and loves to spend her spare time relaxing at the lake.

Made in the USA
Coppell, TX
31 January 2025

45252265R00069